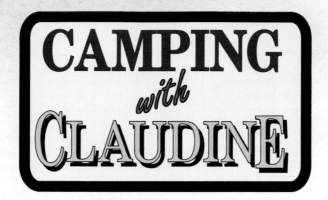

CAMPING
with
CLAUDINE

Written by Virginia King
Illustrated by Bettina Guthridge

Saturday morning

Dear Dad,

We're having a great time
with Aunt Claudine. Today
she's taking us camping!

She says camping is fun,
as long as you take everything
you need.

Millie wanted to take her bike,
but Aunt Claudine said
there wasn't enough room.
I hope we haven't forgotten
anything.

Love from Toby

*P.S. I bet Toby's forgotten
something.*

Love from Millie

MAIL

Saturday afternoon

Dear Dad,

We haven't started camping yet,
but I'm sure we will soon —
after we fix the car.

Aunt Claudine has pulled out
all the parts that need fixing,
and I'm going to help her
put them back.

Millie wants to help, too,
but she doesn't know
how to fix cars.

Love from Toby

*P.S. I don't think Toby can fix
cars either.*

Love from Millie

Sunday morning

Dear Dad,

It was great fun camping by the side of the road last night. We had to unpack the whole car to find the tent. Millie and I were so excited that we giggled all night.

Aunt Claudine says she didn't sleep very well — something must have kept her awake.

The car is working again.

Love from Toby

P.S. I found the part that fixed the car.

Love from Millie

Dear Dad,

It's taking a long time
to find the lake. It's not easy
because a lot of the roads
look exactly the same.

Aunt Claudine thought she had
a map, but we can't find it.

Millie keeps saying that she's
seen these roads before,
but I keep telling her
she's never been to the lake.

Love from Toby

P.S. We're driving around in circles.

Love from Millie

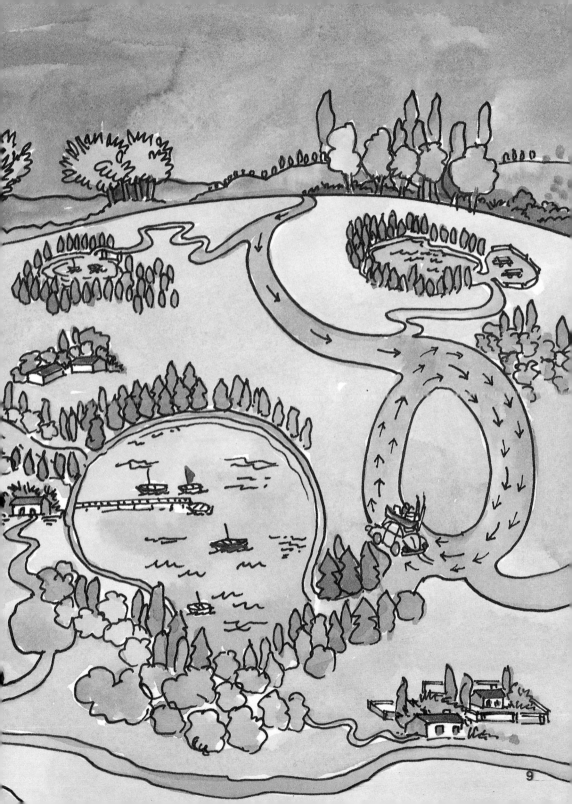

Monday morning

Dear Dad,

We found a lake!

Aunt Claudine says it's not
the lake she was looking for,
but we like it anyway.

It was dark when we arrived,
so we put up the tent right away.
I helped Aunt Claudine,
but Millie didn't.

The tent looked crooked when
we'd finished, but I still think
it's a great tent.

Love from Toby

*P.S. The tent fell down
and we slept in the car.*

Love from Millie

Monday afternoon

Dear Dad,

The lake is great!

Aunt Claudine wanted a rest this afternoon, but we took her out in the canoe instead.

It was fun, except we couldn't find the paddle. Aunt Claudine paddled with her hands.

Now I know what happens when someone stands up in a canoe. Lucky the lake wasn't very deep.

Love from Toby

P.S. Toby stood up and made the canoe tip over.

Love from Millie

Wednesday

Dear Dad,

It's been raining since Monday.
Aunt Claudine said she's sorry
things aren't going very well,
but I told her we're having fun.

Love from Toby

P.S. The tent leaks.

Love from Millie

Thursday

Dear Dad,

We've been in the tent for three days. Time sure goes fast when you're having a good time.

We've had cold baked beans every night, because it's too wet to make a campfire.

I'm glad that cold baked beans taste just as good as hot ones.

Love from Toby

P.S. I don't like cold baked beans.

Love from Millie

Friday

Dear Dad,

It's stopped raining.

We're having fish for dinner.
I like baked beans better.

We went fishing today
and Aunt Claudine showed us
how to use a fishing rod.

I think fishing is boring.

Love from Toby

P.S. I caught six fish
and Toby didn't catch any.

Love from Millie

Saturday

Dear Dad,

Today's our last day at the lake.
Aunt Claudine wanted a rest
so I helped her climb
into the hammock.

Well, I tried. After a while,
Aunt Claudine said she'd sit
on the ground instead.

The hammock is very comfortable
once you get in.

Love from Toby

P.S. Aunt Claudine fell out
of the hammock ten times.

Love from Millie

Sunday

Dear Dad,

We're coming home today.

I asked Aunt Claudine if we could stay for another week, but she said we should leave while we're still enjoying ourselves.

I hope she takes us camping again next year.

Love from Toby

P.S. Aunt Claudine is smiling today.

Love from Millie